Adva[illegible]

One does not usually associate the words "divorce" and "bliss" in the same sentence. Yet, Jude Walsh's book *Post-Divorce Bliss* describes the excitement and transformation that can emerge from facing such an unwanted and unexpected event. She invites the reader to engage in provocative and probing questions that plumb the intricacies of the unsettling experiences that immediately follow a sudden rupture to one's life. She knows firsthand the negative loop that one faces when dealing with the shock of ending one's relationship and facing the task of rearranging their life directions and hopes after an unwanted divorce. Because she knows this terrain well, Jude is always two steps ahead of the reader in supporting those various shaky transitions that such a journey demands. She counteracts each emerging negative and helpless perspective by expanding the reader's world view, and points to the emerging perspectives that are on the cusp on showing itself. In addition she offers practical and life-giving strategies to support the transition into the new. Written in a straight forward, honest style, this book challenges the reader to move bravely through the fires of this life experience towards the spaciousness and brilliant life yet to be discovered.

—Catherine Comuzzi, Ed.D. Cg. Psych
Registered Psychotherapist

Jude Walsh knows what she's talking about – and she expresses herself beautifully. This is a smart, important book written for the person who has no choice but to deal with life after divorce. It is filled with practical knowledge from an excellent coach and I highly recommend it!

—Eric Maisel, *Overcoming Your Difficult Family*
http://www.ericmaisel.com
http://www.ericmaiselsolutions.com
http://www.thefutureofmentalhealth.com

POST-DIVORCE Bliss

Ending Us and Finding Me

JUDE WALSH

NEW YORK

LONDON • NASHVILLE • MELBOURNE • VANCOUVER

POST-DIVORCE *Bliss*

Ending Us and Finding Me

Published in New York, New York, by Morgan James Publishing in partnership with Difference Press. Morgan James is a trademark of Morgan James, LLC.
www.MorganJamesPublishing.com

ISBN 9781642792348 paperback
ISBN 9781642792355 eBook
Library of Congress Control Number: 2018910510

Cover Design by:
Megan Dillon
megan@creativeninjadesigns.com

Interior Design by:
Chris Treccani
www.3dogcreative.net

To all the women recreating themselves post-divorce,
you've got this! Welcome to your second bloom.

And, as always, to my son Brendan, you inspire me.

Table of Contents

Foreword

"This is not the life I ordered," Jude says in the beginning of her book. These seven words will resonate with millions. They capture the experience of mid-life women everywhere who are looking forward to a future of joy and intimacy and then are blindsided by a partner who indicates by his words or deeds that he wants to end their long-term marriage.

Having been through the pain of separation and divorce and coming out the other side to reclaim her lost self, Jude offers guidance for the women who hunger for the support and understanding to bring them through the dark nights of pain and suffering to a life that is more beautiful than anything they have experienced before. Men suffer as well when a marriage ends, but there are unique wounds that women experience that only a woman can truly understand.

I first met Jude in 2002 and was impressed with the personal healing she had done on her own journey of self-discovery and how engaged she was in helping other women navigate difficult relationships to bring clarity to their lives. Her long experiences as an educator allowed her to use her own life experiences as a template and catalyst to tune into the needs of women who were reaching out for help. She was already the go-to person when women wanted to talk about their lives, their loves, and their losses.

And truly, divorce is a loss that rips us apart and can challenge everything we thought we knew about our partner, ourselves, and our future. We need help getting through a divorce at any stage of life, but help is particularly important when we're 40 or older. I wrote three books about my own struggles and the impact these mid-life issues have on the lives of men and women–*Male Menopause, Surviving Male Menopause,* and *The Irritable Male Syndrome.* I learned that mid-life is a difficult life stage for everyone and a separation or divorce during this period of life can be devastating.

Jude has masterfully crafted a book that not only will help women get through the divorce with her body, mind, and spirit intact, but helps women use this life-changing, often traumatic, experience to heal themselves and to create a life based on self-acceptance, joy, and freedom.

Getting through a divorce is like going through the death of a loved one, but it can be even more difficult. When someone dies there's a true ending and we can move more quickly through the stages of loss that Elisabeth Kübler-Ross describes in her book *On Death and Dying:* Denial, anger, bargaining, depression, and acceptance. But when we go through a divorce, particularly if we're the one who didn't want it, we can struggle for years denying that it is over and feel angry about what was done in the past. Our ex may continue to be doing things that are hurtful. Depression may last for months or years and we experience post-traumatic stress that can be triggered over and over again as we must interact with our partner around issues of money, children, support, and a hundred and one details of daily living.

What I find particularly valuable about Jude's book is the simple, yet effective, guidance she provides in helping the reader address all the issues that are so painful and confusing as she moves from a life involving *us* to one created around *me*. You'll identify with Jude's personal story as she confronts her husband's infidelity and the shock and dismay that she was forced to endure.

You'll recognize the questions she must confront:

- Where do I fit?
- What's my support structure now?
- Who can I count on for help?
- Will I have enough money to live?
- What will my future hold?

Jude helps you look back to analyze your marriage so you can better understand what went wrong, what you can learn, and how to come to peace with this painful, but necessary, transition from the world of a married couple to the world of your own emerging self.

You'll be given guided exercises and writing prompts that help you heal at the same time that they guide you through the nitty-gritty activities you must perform to keep your life afloat while you're dealing with confused emotions, painful memories, and longing to have this *be over with already*.

Jude helps bring out your hidden strengths and stands beside you as you own them, develop them, and express them more fully in your life. She helps you deal with the inevitable setbacks that can derail a person when they feel, *finally I've got it figured out and I'm home free.* But you are hit with another one of life's realities and you are forced to go deeper to find hidden sources of courage you never knew you had.

When you begin this journey, it is hard to imagine that you will ever achieve *post-divorce bliss*, but Jude has helped hundreds of women to do just that. I can't think of anyone I know who can give you the support you need to come through divorce a stronger, more loving person, than Jude Walsh. So, jump in and enjoy the ride.

Jed Diamond, Ph.D., author *My Distant Dad: Healing the Family Father Wound, The Enlightened Marriage: The 5 Transformative Stages of Relationship and Why the Best is Still to Come* and *Surviving Male Menopause: A Guide for Women and Men*

Introduction

• • • • • • • • • • • •

This is not the life I ordered. Divorce after a long marriage comes as a shock, disconnecting two people who have been together for most of a lifetime. Some partners accept it easily and move on quickly. Others are blindsided, devastated, deeply wounded. If you are among those, this book is for you.

Divorce is common in the United States. Current statistics estimate 40% of first marriages, 60% of second marriages, and a whopping 70% of third marriages end in divorce. Yet most of us believe when we marry that *our* marriage will last forever. The longer we are married, the more convinced of this we become.

When we say *divorce*, we usually mean the legal dissolution of a marriage. That is one definition, one that is nice, tidy, and devoid of emotion or feeling; a simple legal transaction. Divorce is also defined as a separation between things which were or ought to be connected; to separate or dissociate from something else. It is the second definition that can bring us to our knees.

If betrayal is involved, the wound is particularly deep. How, after all these years together, could this happen? Especially at a time when we have raised our children or built our careers and now have the time to enjoy the fruits of our labor. Did all those years of working together to get here mean nothing? Were we married to strangers? It can feel that way.

It is understandable to refuse to accept this sea change in your life, to believe that it is an aberration, a glitch in an otherwise solid relationship. It is understandable to want to fight to heal the marriage. It is understandable to nurture the hope that your partner will come to his senses, realize what is being destroyed, and do the work necessary to heal and rebuild. When that doesn't happen, when he walks away from the marriage, when your touchstone is no longer yours, when your wealth is suddenly divided, when you are suddenly on your own after a lifetime of together, the trauma can devastate even the strongest among us.

Sometimes we forget how strong we are. We forget how precious and valuable we are. We might lose track of what *we* gave, what we sacrificed, to get to this point. A sacred, not just a legal, contract has been violated. In our pain, we doubt our worth, question our judgment, and no longer trust our power of discernment. We feel discarded. The person who promised to love and honor us until death do us part has reneged. We are expected to just take what we are given and step aside. It's over, we're told; just accept it.

The divorce process is particularly difficult if you were caught unawares by infidelity. While reeling from the discovery, you have the task of creating a new life when you had been happy with the life you had. You enter the territory of taking a long hard look at what you really did have–only this time, without the rose-colored glasses–and this *hurts.* You might for a long while still nurture the hope that he will wake up; he will see what he has destroyed and want to rebuild. But then, perhaps, he might remarry, or you might, in your efforts to heal, realize that you deserve better than what you had.

This experience happens to even the best, the brightest, the most competent, and strong women. We forget our mobility and our ability to problem-solve, and we dwell in the house of pain. We lose our way, our sense of self, our confidence, and our place in the world. Being a wife is a central part of our identity—and then suddenly, it is not. We feel shame, humiliation, regret, grief, and anger.

Our lives are shattered by divorce. We no longer have a partner to depend upon. Our financial status changes: at best we have half of what we had together, and the cold truth is it is often less than half. Our social status changes too. While you were once firmly rooted in a couple-oriented social scene, you are suddenly partnerless and no longer included. This is more painful if your ex has remarried and the new wife just slips into what was once your place. And what about all the traditions you built together over the life of the marriage? What happens on Christmas or other religious holidays? Who is with you to celebrate your birthday, Valentine's Day, achievements in your career? Who is there to care for you if you get sick or experience some other kind of life setback?

You realize the cold hard truth that life as you knew it is over–that it does not matter one bit if this was your wish or is your worst nightmare. It simply is, and living with that hurts. You feel powerless. You might think you have a handle on it and have moved on when something or someone reignites the pain. It might be when close friends celebrate a special anniversary. It might be seeing a couple walking hand-in-hand. It might be getting a Christmas letter from a friend telling you how wonderful and perfect their married life is.

While these might be the most painful times of all, it is also the time when the light breaks through. This might not be the life you ordered, but it can be a pathway to the life you deserve. And the life you deserve is better, brighter, more fulfilling than you imagined possible. You can move from feeling you *have* to start over to rejoicing that you *get* to start over.

I can help you travel this path.

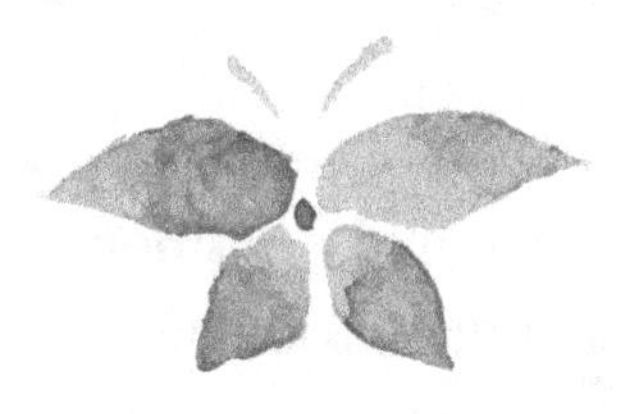

Chapter 1

My Story

On July 1, 1972, I married my high school sweetheart and beau of six years. We had graduated from college a few weeks earlier and were thrilled to be starting our married life. When he was accepted to law school two years later, we moved from my birthplace, surrounded by my beloved mountains, to the Midwest. I left a beautiful teaching position to move to Dayton, Ohio, with no job prospects and worry about how I was going to support us while he studied. On the day I finally found a position, we were down to five dollars in cash, but we had one another and that was all we needed to succeed.

I married my best friend and soul mate. I always joked that it never mattered who else was at a party because I came with the most interesting person there. Any life challenge that came our way was surmountable because we faced it together. As long as we had each other, we could do anything.

He promised me we would return home after law school, but his best job opportunity was in Dayton and we had made friends there, so we stayed. Life was good. He had a job at a prominent law firm, and I gave birth to our first and only child, a son. Our son had numerous and complex health and developmental problems. I worked part-time because our son was frequently hospitalized and one parent had to be available. My husband was on a partnership track and worked long hours. Our son's illness had no impact on his career because I was there. Not having more children is my single greatest life regret.

The years flew by. My husband made partner at his law firm. I completed a master's degree and then received a full scholarship to complete my doctorate. We were debt-free, financially stable, and blessed with friends and family. Our son's health improved and we were finally able to do the traveling we both loved. I could commit to my career for the first time. I embraced my profession, teaching students with multiple disabilities and language disorders at an elementary school during the day and a course I designed for the local university at night. Then an amazing and innovative group of teachers approached me to help co-found a charter school. For the first time in our married life, I focused on my career and was at my most creative and happiest professionally.

At first, my husband seemed thrilled and supportive. Then I noticed a subtle change. He would make an occasional snarky remark about the cohesiveness of our staff. This was a shock, because in all 30 years of our marriage there was rarely a cross or critical word between us. He became more irritable. I decided he must be having a midlife crisis and that maybe my success was bothering him. This was the best man I knew, my life mate, father to my son, and my greatest love. I decided to just grant him grace and love him through it.

That became more difficult when I discovered his infidelity. My husband, my soul mate, had a secret life. And he was not at all sure he was willing to give it up. The person I trusted most in the world had been lying to me constantly, about even the most trivial things. When I found out I was so traumatized I began to vomit, couldn't sleep, could not focus. I lost 90 pounds.

I kept his affair a secret. I was so ashamed that my perfect marriage was a farce, so humiliated. I believed he would come to his senses at some point, the midlife crisis would pass, and we could heal the hurts. I loved him enough to try.

He swore the affair was over and he was committed to repairing our marriage and we began therapy. Six months into therapy I discovered he had maintained contact with her the entire time we were trying to put the marriage back together. He moved out, and I stopped keeping the affair a secret. Over the next year, I tried to heal our marriage with him.

When I realized that marriage repair took two and he was ambivalent, I began to work on healing me instead.

In addition to anxiety, one of the trauma symptoms I experienced was an inability to read. I could recognize the words but could glean no meaning from them. This made grant reading and writing, planning professional development, and creating written communication for my school difficult. I was one of the two school leaders, and I was now unreliable at best. At the same time, my mother's health began to fail. Something had to give.

My therapist warned me that if I did not change something that, in addition to my mental health, my physical health would suffer. I had to choose between my marriage and my career, and I chose my marriage. I left my most-loved job. I had enough years in to retire but lost ten extra years of earned income and consequently have a much lower retirement income than I would have if I had stayed and worked in the school I treasured.

Over the next few years I committed myself to every healing strategy I could find. After my husband quit couples' therapy, I continued therapy on my own. I found an international expert on surviving the behavior associated with male menopause and began what would be many years of counseling. After being diagnosed with PTSD, I relied on medication for anxiety and depression until I was able to sleep again. I began to exercise compulsively, but worked to change that into healthy exercise habits. I used alternative healing methods like eye movement desensitization and reprocessing (EMDR) and tapping. I joined 12-step groups for partners of sex addicts and codependents. I had always put others' needs before my own, but finally through my healing efforts learned that selfish and self-care are not the same thing.

Once the news was out, friendships changed. Many people were at first sympathetic, shocked by my husband's behavior. As time passed they became frustrated that we did not either divorce or get back together. He was telling me he needed more time and was trying to work out his problems, and I was patient. I did not know he was dating, and none of my supposed friends thought to tell me. I was not dating or even thinking about it because I was still married. Those vows meant something to me. When the judge at our divorce hearing remarked that my husband must want to get remarried as he was rushing the divorce proceedings, those words surprised me. I did not know he was in a relationship. We did not divorce until he found someone else to marry.

It was a seven-year journey from discovery to divorce. I'd like to tell you the divorce granted me clarity, but it was only another step. It took a few more years of therapy, 12-step work, and commitment to a new life before I finally felt truly happy again.

And happy I am! I work at two things I love as much as I loved teaching and creating a new school: being a writer and a life coach. I have taken every bit of what I learned and applied it first to my life and now to helping other women get to this blissful place faster and easier than I did. I wake up every day full of plans, connections, and delight. I satisfy my wanderlust on a regular basis, often combining travel with writing and coaching. I love exercise and do it in a healthy way, walking, hiking, and dancing with a tribe of fellow fitness enthusiasts. I revel in being responsible for my own finances and life planning and have an excellent support team. I am doing things I never imagined I would.

If you are in the space between leaving your marriage behind and the next step, ready to move forward but not exactly sure how, this book is for you. This is the book I wish I'd had. I want you to experience the same growth I have, but more easily and in less time. The following chapters include questions and writing prompts as action steps. Let's begin.

Chapter 2

Shifting Perspective

A divorce is a legal document; it captures a moment in time. While you are not technically divorced until the document is filed, once you sign that document and walk out of the courthouse, you are no longer a wife. A role that was an integral part of your identity is swept away. You are no longer half of a couple. You are no longer married. You now have to check the box that says *divorced* when asked for your marital status. That's the legal part.

The experience is so much more than that. Signing divorce papers does not magically make all the pain and hurt and complicated feelings leave.

- What happens to your emotions?
- What happens to your sense of self?
- What happens to your social status?
- Where do you fit?
- What is your support structure now?
- Whom can you count on for help if you need it?
- What about finances? Your standard of living just changed dramatically. The future that you planned with two incomes is gone. Can you maintain your lifestyle?
- What will your future hold? Even if you are relieved that the divorce struggle is finally over, you now have to plan solo.
- Did you perhaps think right up until the moment the papers were signed that this might go away–that you might get your life back?

- Are you still appalled that your soon-to-be-ex is treating you this way?
- Do you feel like you were thrown under the bus so he could have what he wanted?
- Are you harboring some doubts about your own worth since your identity has been changed?
- Do you have low self-esteem?
- What about your body image?
- What do you do to curb the anxiety?
- Do you need new ways to celebrate holidays and special occasions?
- How do you make the journey from wife to single woman in the most affirming, uplifting way?

You are a smart, capable, talented, beautiful, desirable woman (although you may not believe it at the moment) who has just experienced one of *the* most stressful life changes. Expect to experience very normal mood swings, vacillating between relief and grief, sadness and euphoria, fear and unbridled optimism, hope and hopelessness, relishing your freedom and worrying about loneliness, grieving the end and anticipating beginning anew, feeling out of control and empowered to do anything.

You may feel as if part of your life has been severed, like a limb amputation. For a long time you may experience phantom pain, feeling the wife part when you know that piece of you is gone. But you are a starfish. That severed arm will grow back, and you will be stronger and more beautiful than ever.

Creating a new life is not a linear process. We are beginning the journey to the top of the mountain; there is more than one way to get there. You may take switchbacks that leave you feeling like you are working hard to go a short distance. You may occasionally veer off onto a side path to rest and enjoy the scenery. You may meet some fellow travelers and decide to stop and play and learn with them for a while. You may put your head down and just trudge onward. You may decide to create a new route on the trail, leaving blaze marks for those following.

I'll walk beside you, holding your hand, pulling you up when stuck, pointing out the rocks and drop-offs, allowing you alone time as needed and chat time when desired. It's your journey, only you can choose the way.

I'm here as a guide to help you navigate the trip. I've done it, and I can affirm it is so beautiful at the top. Clean fresh air, spectacular views, that powerful feeling you get when you've done something hard and done it well. We are going to take this one step at a time. Each of the following topics will offer you a way forward to create the life you desire and deserve.

- Marriage autopsy: An invitation to decide what to take from the marriage and what to give a peaceful burial
- Go beyond grief: Information about grieving and techniques for dealing with the loss and sadness of divorce
- Transform your trauma: Strategies for coping with trauma triggers
- Balance your body: Advice about reclaiming your body, treating it well, and reveling in it
- Manage your money: Thoughts on changing your mindset around money–accept your power, learning to see money as energy, and developing an abundance mindset

- Discover your tribe: Stories and tips about how to start, deepen, and appreciate relationships with your tribe
- Create new traditions: Ideas for creating new ways to celebrate holidays that are more in keeping with your new life
- Re-story your life: Steps toward formalizing the plan for your new life
- Moving ahead: thoughts on taking your next steps

Not only have I traveled this path, but I've also helped many other women find post-divorce bliss. I know these steps really can help you on your journey. Your time is now.

Chapter 3

Marriage Autopsy

The marriage is dead. It is time to do an autopsy, to see what happened and what can be learned. The word autopsy is derived from the Greek word *autoptes*, "eyewitness" from *autos*–self–and *optos*–seen. Literally a way of self-seeing. It is time to witness your marriage and make new meaning.

Perhaps you are still stunned that your marriage is over, unsure of what really happened. Maybe you are thrilled to finally have it behind you. Possibly you fluctuate between mourning its end and being angry and resentful that it died. You are wondering if all those years were wasted. All understandably human!

We tend to vacillate between two lenses when looking back. The first is the filter of pain that taints everything, that makes you unable to remember the marriage without regret and sadness, doubting that any of the good was real. The other perspective is when you've taken off the rose-colored glasses you used most of your married life and are appalled and filled with regret at what you didn't see, blaming and shaming yourself. Let's go to both those places, dig into the body of the marriage and determine what was healthy and what was diseased. Once you have a clear picture of what worked and what didn't, you can rebuild. You can take all the good and use it for creation.

Let's start by remembering what was good. We all enter our marriages with love and hope and promise. We have found our mate, our match, and plan to build our life together. We brought our best self to the marriage and saw the best in our partner. That partner changed, is no longer who you believed him to be. Maybe he never was; maybe he just became someone else that you now don't like or trust. Perhaps you have changed as well. At the moment it feels like wasted years. But let's take a look.

Take a few minutes to answer each of these questions. Find a quiet spot and carve out some time. Perhaps light a candle and make yourself a mug of tea or glass of wine. Create a safe space. Maybe get out your wedding album or honeymoon pictures. Allow the feelings to flow. There are no right or wrong answers, only seeking knowledge.

- What was the best strength you brought to the marriage?
- In what ways were you supportive of your partner and his life goals?
- Name your five favorite moments together. What made them special?
- Relive your wedding day, especially your vows. Note how you honored them.
- When were you there for your partner when he needed you most? How did you do that?
- Name five things he did for you that you loved and why you deserved them.

- Now spend some time thinking about all the good you brought to this union. All of that good is still in you. Write a statement describing that woman.

Now let's summon up the courage and look at what you did that contributed to the end of the marriage or what you refused to see that might have served as an early warning. Be gentle with yourself, practice compassion. We all make mistakes. We all have things we regret. But the best among us recognize those and learn from them. It is possible to learn and forgive and grow. It is possible to move on with lightness in your heart. Let's look at what went wrong, what wasn't seen. When you look back from the perspective of the marriage having failed, you can sometimes see what went wrong and what was missed. Recreate that space you designed for your first exercise or create another spot. Just be sure to be comfortable and have some uninterrupted private time. Then respond to these prompts.

- Now that you have some hindsight, what is the one big sign you missed? Why did you miss it?

- Was there something about your ex that made you uncomfortable from the start? What made you decide to overlook it?
- Describe a few instances in which you were hurt or annoyed or disrespected and you said nothing.
- What attributes did he have that made you overlook his flaws?
- Did you stay too long, after you knew it was no longer good for you? If so, why?
- What kept you from confronting the problem earlier?

Now look at each of those things and write a statement of forgiveness and understanding about it. Then release them knowing you have learned. For example: *I gave my very best to my marriage and I forgive myself for any mistakes I made. Looking back I can see I tolerated things that were not good for me; I realize that now and will move forward with more awareness.*

Finally, let's put this autopsy into perspective and assign new meaning. All of the things that went wrong or that you felt you didn't handle well can be buried now. They will gently decompose, making compost, creating fertile ground. The ground may lie fallow for a season or two, but eventually something will burst forth. All the strengths and good things noted in the first exercise will fuel this phoenix rising. You are on your way. You are creating something new and beautiful and filled with promise. When you make another mistake, or take a wrong turn, remember what you have written today. You are strong and your mistakes are just fodder for the soil, fertilizing and fueling a glorious second bloom.

Chapter 4

Go Beyond Grief

Divorce is death–the death of a marriage. Whether you have divorced amicably or acrimoniously, that relationship is finished. You can't redo it. You can't make it grow. You can't give it a new life. The marriage is dead and with death comes grief. Elizabeth Kubler-Ross first described the five stages of grief she observed in her work with terminally ill people as denial, anger, bargaining, depression, and acceptance. She was criticized when it was assumed she meant all people experience all these stages in that exact order. We now know people can experience some but not all stages and that grief can come in waves or cycles. When comparing divorce to death it is easy to see the stages present themselves, especially in the court proceedings, ending with accepting the final decree.

The other misperception fostered by the concept of steps is assuming that once you have passed though the stages you are finished and then you should "be fine," "move on," "stop talking about it." People might give a widow some slack here, but divorced women are expected to move on quickly. If you are openly suffering or grieving for too long, you can expect unwanted advice about how to get over him. "Date again." "Get laid." "Spend money on yourself." Or you might experience another painful possibility–shunning. When this happens, people will start to avoid you, deliberately leave you out of groups, stop inviting you to parties. They'll no longer want to listen when you want to talk about your marriage. There will be the shifting away of eye contact, the sudden change of topic, or the glances of frustration between your friends. They may think that allowing you to keep talking is enabling you to stay stuck when all you want to do is mourn a little. They may step away. And then you begin grieving the loss of those friendships as well as the loss of your marriage.

Lisa felt isolated after her divorce. On the surface it looked like she was coping well, moving on. But she was relying too heavily on work, pouring herself into every task, taking work home to fill some of the hours in the evening. She was avoiding being social with her colleagues–she did not want to hear about their happy personal lives. As a consequence, people were leaving her pretty much alone. When her supervisor stopped by her desk one day to congratulate her on doing such good work, her response was to burst into tears. It felt like the first kind words she had heard in forever, and it overwhelmed her.

The grief she had been pushing down surfaced. She was embarrassed, but this outburst turned out to be good for her. We put together some strategies, a sort of go-to list that she kept in her purse to help her recognize when she was feeling sad or overwhelmed. We also made a plan for her to seek out someone at work as an ally in the process.

Once she stopped denying the feelings, started allowing them to surface before they reached such an intense place, she could feel them, soothe herself, and stay more present with her colleagues. To her surprise, a co-worker reached out, sharing her story of a relationship gone wrong and her loneliness. The two women made a pact to meet after work once a week for dinner. They promised to listen to one another with the caveat that what was expressed must be productive grief. They created a judgment-free two-person grief support group that morphed into genuine friendship.

Many women say that it would be easier to be widowed than divorced. As a widow, you may have lost his income, but you still retain all your assets. Divorce court, on the other hand, can be combative, and the one with the best lawyer wins. If there is not an equitable distribution of assets when a man and a woman split up, it is usually the woman who suffers. It is painful to have the person you trusted most in the world trying to grab as much as he can for himself, and keep as much away from you as possible. That cuts to the heart. The grief over that is huge and will resurface every time you realize you can no longer afford something.

A widow keeps intact her memories of a lasting relationship. She knows her husband loved and treasured her until the day he died. In divorce, you have been rejected, deemed no longer the right choice for a life partner.

If betrayal was involved in the end of your marriage, many people will have difficulty understanding why you have any sadness at all. Well-meaning people will tell you that you are better off without him, that he was never who you thought he was, and that you deserve better. Even if all of that is true, he was still the person you loved and trusted and the person you planned a future with. The shift away from him is wrenching and marks a loss of trust, a loss of a sense of safety in the world. You are not just grieving the marriage; you are grieving the loss of what might have been.

The combination of loss and then guilt for still feeling the loss can bring deep sadness. It is important to allow yourself to feel those feelings. It is normal to think it might have been easier to be widowed. It is normal to resent your changed financial status. As you rebuild your life these feelings will fade, replaced by an emphasis on what you have rather than what was lost.

Grief can be triggered in myriad ways. Maybe you get an invitation to a 25th wedding anniversary party, and you realize you'll never hit that mark. Perhaps someone's spouse is throwing them a special birthday party, and you realize you have no spouse to do that for you. Maybe you are filling out a form and you have to check off the box marked *divorced* and are suddenly unsure who your person to call in case of emergency is now. Sometimes it is watching your peers move into retirement together and seeing them fulfill the kind of plans you once had with your ex. Maybe it is noticing your ex does the exact kind of special things for his new wife that he used to do for you. That triggers the grief of realizing that perhaps there was nothing special about the two of you. Wife seems to just be a slot to be filled, interchangeable. You grieve the loss of the magic.

Rather than avoiding grief, you can embrace it as a healing thing. When you fall into grief your eyes and heart and emotions momentarily open again, and this can take you to a deeper level of healing. A person, a body, a spirit, can only tolerate so much grief at one time; that is one reason why it comes in waves. As we can handle more, we get more. Know that grief is normal. You've lost something very precious to you, and it is going to take a long time to feel okay. There may always be a well of grief deep within you about the loss of your marriage.

If you're still experiencing grief, it does not mean that you've not moved on; it does not mean he still has power over you. It does not mean you're weak. It does not mean you haven't done the work. It does not mean you're not ready for another relationship. It does not mean you can't move on. It does not mean you're a failure. It does not mean you are too wounded to ever find another partner. It doesn't mean any of that. It shows that you had a deep, deep wound and that you're being given another opportunity to heal at a deeper level still.

Grief may reappear even if you have already moved on and are in a new relationship. It does not mean that your new relationship isn't working. It just means you are again reminded of something you lost. That it was a precious something because you valued it, and because it is precious it will be mourned.

Many times when you're grieving, you're grieving for what might have been. Grief is as much about the future as it is about the past. You thought you were going to have a life together with this person, and you don't. It's just gone. It can be very hurtful to see him living the life you planned with him with someone else, even if you have no desire to be with him again. You might feel you were just a placeholder, that you weren't important. As if you were an actor in the play of his life and he just decided you didn't fit the role anymore.

So what to do when grief strikes?

- Notice and acknowledge it.
- Accept that it has returned.
- Know that it is part of your continued growth.
- Allow yourself to feel whatever it is you need to feel.
- Cut yourself some slack.
- Practice self-care.
- If you desire, talk to someone about it.
- Allow yourself as much time as you need to process it.
- Congratulate yourself on your awareness.
- Surround yourself with people you love. Accept their understanding.

- Count the blessings in your life.
- Allow yourself to feel joy.

Journaling Prompts

- *Today I am experiencing grief. I feel…*
- *When people do not allow me to express or show my grief I am…*
- *Grief is normal. The ways I support myself during this feeling are…*

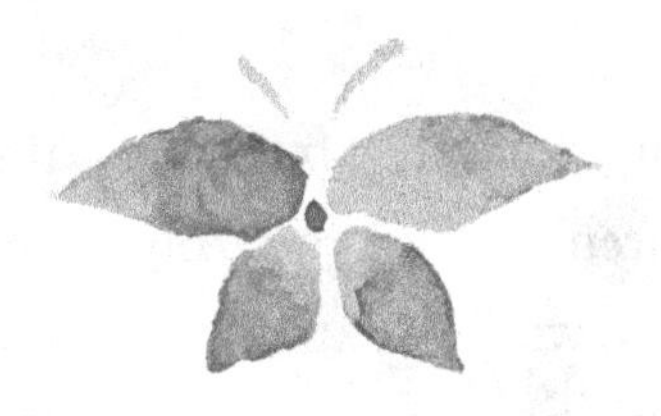

Chapter 5

Transform Your Trauma

Most lists of the most stressful experiences in life identify divorce as number two, second only to the death of a spouse. There is no doubt that getting divorced is traumatic. Even if it is amicable, there are still the stressors of change in living situation, change in income, shifting of social circles, disappointment that the marriage did not survive, changes in parenting, negotiating new relationships with former in-laws, self-examination about what your contribution to the failure was, trying to figure out what mistakes you made in choosing your partner to avoid making them again, perhaps feelings of rejection, concerns about your ability to attract a new partner, and trying to decide if you even want a new partner. Whew! And you have to deal with the legal system, a stress all on its own. Courts and lawyers should come with warning stickers. Have you ever heard someone say how much they enjoyed divorce court? These are all things that can take time to process and time to heal from, but they are manageable.

Once the divorce is over and you think you are home free, it can be disheartening, discouraging, even frightening to find yourself suddenly turned inside out by some reminder of your marriage or the reasons for its demise. That is the time to immerse yourself in self-care. I don't mean just take a few minutes alone or do some deep breathing or repeat a few mantras, though all of those things are lovely and good. When you are recovering from divorce trauma, you need to bring out the big guns, and in order to do that effectively you need to be prepared.

Your assignment is to brainstorm–instead of 50 ways to leave your lover (You only needed one way to do that and it's done!), 50 ways to celebrate you. Get out pen and paper and get creative. Do not stop until you have 50 things on your list, from the ridiculous to the sublime. If you are worried that you cannot do this on your own, call in your friends. Let them know what you are doing and why; invite them over for a pizza or cupcake party and get their help. Actually, calling your friends over for an impromptu party can be number one on your list. I've given you one, now get cracking on 49 more.

Sometimes recovery is more complex, exponentially more difficult, if the divorce circumstances elevate the trauma to a level where you have PTSD. Those situations often involve betrayal of some sort. Perhaps it was an affair, a secret life, lying, misuse of family money, or some other form of deception. Frequently addiction is involved: alcohol, drugs, gambling, or sex. It is most traumatic when the betrayed spouse is blindsided when the truth comes to light.

There are wide variations in what is considered PTSD. One set of criteria says the person's life has to have been threatened. We are all familiar with the many veterans who return from war zones with PTSD. We recognize it in people who have survived genocide or bombings or life-threatening natural disasters like a tornado or earthquake. Victims of sexual assault often have PTSD. Most recently in the U.S. we have had the sad outcome of seeing children who survived school shootings exhibit PTSD. I say exhibit because PTSD shows up when the victim experiences a trigger, something that reminds them of the trauma. The original trauma can be a single incident, something as horrific as a rape or witnessing a murder. Or it can be the result of prolonged experiences, like those of soldiers who are in extended battle situations. We have all heard stories of veterans diving behind bushes when a car backfires. Some assault victims cannot tolerate touch.

The PTSD responses to a trigger are: flight, fight, or freeze. Those are very accurate descriptions. *Flight* might be a physical response–the person literally runs away. It can also be an emotional response in which the person "flees" by entering a dissociative state.

People who have been repeatedly brutalized will talk about leaving their bodies during assault, emotionally distancing themselves from the horror. *Fight* can look like lots of things. Someone might punch, kick, scratch, bite, scream and wave their arms, in an over-the-top, desperate way. Sometimes the fight response is a verbal one–yelling at the person who is triggering the response. *Freeze* can be a bit harder to identify. The person may stop talking, stop interacting, feel helpless to either fight or flee. Sometimes a person experiencing the freeze reaction will have a haunted or desperate look upon their face. Sometimes if you speak to them they are unable to respond. It is a peculiar form of helplessness, of feeling very victimized.

Maybe you have experienced one or more of these responses. Perhaps you had a moment in divorce court where you literally could not respond to a triggering question. Perhaps you found yourself fleeing a social situation when suddenly faced with your ex. Perhaps you snapped a response to what may have seemed like an innocuous question.

I am discussing these responses in detail because I have experienced all of them as a result of the shock of discovering my husband had a secret life, that he was not only betraying me but, if his mistress would have him, was prepared to abandon his family for her. I was blindsided. My life was not in physical danger at that moment of discovery, but I can tell you I thought it was over. The repeated assaults on my sense of safety continued as his lies and betrayals went on. I could no longer trust him and I could no longer trust my discernment about what was real. Court was so traumatizing that to this day I drive alternate streets in the downtown area to avoid the courthouse. I was hypervigilant, another trait shared by combat victims. I could not eat. I could not sleep. I could not relax. I could not focus on conversations. I never felt safe, not for one minute, and required medical care and medication.

My physical health suffered. In addition to vomiting, extreme rapid weight loss, gall bladder surgery, anxiety attacks, and depression, I got breast cancer. Years after the inciting incident, I was still easily triggered. It was not until I divorced and stopped contact with my ex that I began to truly heal.

PTSD is serious and requires both therapy and medical attention. Once I had medication to help me sleep, and to control the anxiety and depression, I made some progress with traditional talk therapy. When I added work with a therapist who used eye movement desensitization and reprocessing (EMDR) and tapping, I improved even more. Trauma memories can be trapped in your body, and those two techniques helped release it.

A truly beneficial thing is to have friends who know what you experience when you are triggered and are willing to either come and get you or talk with you by phone until you feel safe again. Sophie and Julie, members of the support group, agreed to be "on call" for one another. They agreed to call each other when triggered and start the conversation by saying, "I need..." and filling in whatever the need was. Sometimes it was "I just need to process something. Can you listen for a while?" It might be, "I need help right now. Can you come?" Or maybe "I am feeling frightened. Can you talk to me until I feel safe again?" The person called did not offer solutions, only responded as requested. They became so skilled at assisting one another that the calls only lasted a few minutes. Getting support immediately shortens the trauma response. Pairing these two women benefited each of them. They now have a close friendship and only occasionally need a trigger support call. But they know the other person is there if needed.

PTSD does not ever really go away. Many therapists will dispute that, but not many people with PTSD will. I can attest to learning effective strategies to use when triggered. I can attest to being far less frequently or easily triggered. I can also attest to the fact that I can still be triggered. It does not matter that my life was not physically threatened; it was clear to me that my life as I lived it was in danger and I felt powerless to protect myself. If you are experiencing any of the symptoms I have described, get medical and therapeutic help. Do not hesitate. Do not think you can fix this on your own or by talking to friends. Friends can be supportive, but for PTSD you also need expert care. Get it. You are worth it, you deserve it, and you can feel better.

Trauma and PTSD *can* be managed. Just recognizing what you are experiencing is freeing. Know that the trauma response is common and that you are not alone. And know that many others have come out on the other side stronger and open to a relaxed and joyous life. Once you have the tools and strategies necessary, you will cope and compensate quicker and more easily. You will relax into the world and enjoy without anxiety the new experiences you are creating post-divorce.

Journaling Prompts

- Make a gratitude list of all the support you have received to help cope with trauma. Compose a thank-you letter to someone who has helped you.
- Note three situations in which you were triggered. How did you cope? What were some other possible strategies you could use? Remember to congratulate yourself for getting through it.
- Create three mantras to use when triggered.

Chapter 6

Balance Your Body

Women's bodies are ground zero in divorce; they are the terrain that records every battle. This terrain reflects the physical health of and the emotional beliefs we hold about our bodies. At first it is the physical that demands our attention, but, to heal completely, we must also pay attention to our mindset.

Many of us reflect the pain and loss of our marriage within our bodies. Over time, that trauma has long-term effects. Some of us gain weight. Some of us lose weight. Some of us get ulcers. Far too many of us get breast cancer. Acute trauma can deliver an immediate physical impact. Often when women share their stories about either discovering their husband's infidelity or first hearing him say the word *divorce,* they report throwing up. Some women continue to vomit for days or weeks, resulting in dramatic weight loss. Too-rapid weight loss can lead, for example, to gall bladder problems.

I help my clients find healthier ways to relieve stress or tension. Exercise is an excellent solution. Being in motion helps dissipate anxiety and helps tire the body for sleep. If you have a favorite sport or activity, now is the time to increase your level of participation. If you are not athletic, walking is a perfect choice. All you need is a good pair of shoes and some good-quality socks. You can walk in parks and enjoy the added benefit of surrounding yourself with nature. You can walk at the mall and window shop. You can walk on tracks. You can walk around your neighborhood, perhaps meeting some folks you would not have met if you were not on foot. It's a portable physical activity. The first thing my clients notice about walking is that, even when they're very anxious and stressed, if they walk long enough, at a brisk enough pace, endorphins kick in and they start to feel better. That is invaluable, providing relief just when they need it most.

If you are new to exercise, start small, maybe a couple of times around the block. If you can recruit a walking buddy, now is a perfect time to do so. Note your times, distance, and physical and emotional state before and after walking. Most smartphones come with health apps included or available for purchase. If you prefer pen and paper, buy a special journal just for fitness notes. The accumulation of miles is satisfying. Set an audacious goal, for example 500 miles. That might feel outrageous, but if you are walking often to ameliorate stress, miles will mount up quickly. Or choose a place you'd like to go, check how many miles it is to get there, and aim to walk that many miles. If you'd love a vacation in Orlando, Florida, and it is 150 miles from your home, aim to walk that many miles. And then, of course, you will have to walk back!

My client Megan agreed to try walking. She went from huffing and puffing her way around that first block to doing three miles before work in the morning. We registered her for a 5K walk. She really worried over it, afraid she could not keep up with the pack, afraid she would be the very last to cross the finish line. A 5K is only 3.1 miles. She was already walking three miles every day on her own.

She was thrilled to get her first race tee-shirt and line up with the other walkers. She was definitely not last, and stayed at the finish line to cheer on the walkers coming in after she did. She was hooked. She went from 5Ks to 10Ks and eventually completed a half-marathon in the top 25 percent. Today she continues to walk, both for pleasure and for her health. She enjoys the camaraderie of walkers and runners and easily maintains a healthy weight. Her body is a source of pleasure and strength rather than pain. The activity she began to help her cope with divorce trauma is now something she can't live without.

Leann was a plus-size woman struggling after her divorce. She could not sleep and was stress eating. I suggested starting with water aerobics, as it is easier on your joints. It was hard for her to commit to buying a swimsuit and even harder for her to put it on and enter the pool. She didn't like the first class. She had trouble following the instructions, the water was too cold, the other women didn't seem very friendly; she had a litany of complaints. But she agreed to stick it out for the ten-session class.

Once she showed up a few times, the other ladies began to talk to her. She got the moves down and no longer struggled to keep up. When they issued an invitation to meet for pizza after the final class, she went, getting to know her classmates and making a few new friends–friends who only knew her as a single woman. And she kept going to water aerobics. As she became less stressed about her divorce, she was also becoming more attached to exercise.

She noticed a Zumba class that began just as she was leaving water aerobics. One day she stayed and watched it. The instructor invited her to come and try a session. She went, with the caveat that she would only stay as long as she felt she could keep up. The instructor agreed, suggesting that if she tired, she could just march in place for a bit. Leann did not want to do that. She thought that would make her look like a failure but leaving early would not.

She went to the class and spent the first part tripping over her own feet trying to keep up with the steps. At a brief water break, as she was trying to sneak out, several of the women welcomed her and confided that they too felt clumsy and awkward at first. But, they said, it gets better and is really fun. She relaxed and laughed her way through the rest of that class, and felt proud that she not only finished but also had fun. She now wears a regular-sized swimsuit and spandex pants to Zumba. Her divorce seems far behind her as she embraces an active lifestyle. She's gained new friends, a more muscled body, and confidence. And she sleeps like a baby.

Our bodies are negatively affected by stress-related sleep disruption. Constant thinking about marital problems can keep us tossing and turning or, if we do manage to sleep, interrupt that sleep with frequent awakenings. The rejuvenation and replenishment that occurs during normal sleep is lost. Sleep deprivation can result in memory and thinking difficulties, increased inflammation that raises the risk of diabetes and heart problems, weight gain, and heightened risk for accidents.

If the sleep loss is extreme, you may need to seek help from a physician.

Listening to a relaxation recording or a meditation track can help. Also try diffusing relaxing essential oils, such as lavender. Having beautiful sheets and spreads and comfortable pillows helps. Set a regular bedtime and turn off all electronics an hour or so before bed. Some of my clients set up a goodnight call from a good friend. It is nice to hear a loving voice before bed.

If you can't sleep, try getting out of bed, writing down whatever is bothering you, and then ripping the paper into the tiniest possible pieces and throwing them away. Try this mantra: *I release these troubles; they bother me no more as I drift into a peaceful sleep.* Or create a mantra that feels right to you. The goal is to establish a routine that gives you maximum potential for a restful night. As difficult as these sleep-troubled nights are, they will diminish over time. Exercise can help here too.

One of the most dangerous physical complications of divorce is breast cancer. I was diagnosed with Paget's disease of the breast, an unusual cancer. Part of the treatment plan was a session with a social worker. She asked what was going on in my life, and I told her about the affair, the dramatic weight loss, the treatment for PTSD, the gall bladder surgery, and the ongoing marital conflict.

She asked me if I had been abused, and I said no. As I answered her, I flashed back to a desperate conversation I had had with my husband in which I'd said, "Just hit me." He was appalled: "I would never hit you." My response was, "Just hit me. People would understand that." I knew a black eye or a bruise is obvious; emotional abuse is not so easily, or willingly, recognized.

The social worker explained to me that she sees stress-related cancers all the time. She told me bluntly, "You have to start telling yourself the truth. You were abused, and abused badly. Your body knows, and unless you start telling the truth, you will have more problems."

I was stunned. I realized that not only was my body the battleground for this marital conflict, but it was a barometer of truth. I vowed in that moment to stop denying what was right in front of me. I decided to stop giving my ex a pass for his behavior and continuing emotional abuse. That is the moment I began to heal both physically and emotionally.

I never forgot that lesson from the social worker, and it paid off for my client Janet. When we designed a plan for her as she was exiting her marriage, I suggested she have a mammogram. She didn't want to do that; she felt she had too much on her plate between depositions and appointments with her lawyer and making new living arrangements. But self-care was part of the plan, so she agreed. The mammogram revealed a small lump that was removed in an outpatient procedure. It was her wake-up call to pay more attention to her body. She chose bicycling, as she liked being outdoors. She has since remarried a fine fellow she met while cycling, and she and her new husband take bicycling vacations all across the United States.

Body shaming complicates the process of healing from divorce. Unfortunately women sometimes shame each other. I recall one woman commenting, when she had heard that someone else's husband was unfaithful, "but she's not even fat"–as if a man gets a pass on cheating if his partner is overweight, or that infidelity is all a "fat" woman deserves. When Christie Brinkley's husband cheated on her with their nanny, many women were perplexed because she's *Christie Brinkley*. She was a model and still looked amazing (unspoken rest of the sentence: "for her age.") How could he possibly cheat on her? Well, because it was not about her appearance.

Those kind of toxic ideas slip into our worldviews and have to be deconstructed for what they are: judgmental and cruel. I encourage all women to speak up when they hear an unkind body judgment from another woman. If you speak up, that clearing of the air, that calling out of comments that are unkind or cruel, helps not just your state of mind but the mindset of all women.

Body shaming can also come from a woman's partner. If the wife is overweight or if she's too thin her partner might say, "Well, you know I'm just not into you. I love you but I'm not *in love* with you." Or perhaps he shares that he wants out of the marriage because he is no longer physically attracted to you. You may know intellectually that he is just excusing his own bad behavior, but in your heart and mind you register that the problem is your body. This leads to all kinds of negative thoughts.

If I change my body I can save my marriage. If I lose weight he will be attracted to me again. If I lose weight then he'll remember me from when we first fell in love and fall in love with me again. If I change my body, I'll be attractive to the world in general, and then he'll be proud of me and want to keep me as his wife. Or, *if I gain weight, I'll be curvier or have bigger breasts and that will please him.*

Tara struggled with her feelings about her plus-size body after her husband had an affair with a very petite woman. She felt like she could never be that small or that thin. She just felt wrong. We looked at magazines together and noted more voluptuous models in them, but that didn't soothe her pain or boost her self-image. She noted that those "plus-size" models were no more than a size 16, and she was well above that.

What did help was an assignment to go to a Renaissance fair. Many women there are beyond voluptuous and are saucy wenches, very body confident! She saw heavier women flaunting their curves and men of all sizes and ages appreciating them. She's become a weekend "Rennie" and is having the time of her life.

As for me, the more comfortable I became in my body, the more confidence I gained. Increasing my physical strength gave me emotional strength. I learned to tune into my body for its wisdom, something I had never done before. I was always intuitive but this was different. The exercise empowered me in a way that all the talk therapy, medical treatment for PTSD, and 12-step work did not.

Physical activity serves me well in my new life. Because I am fit I can do things like hike Mount Cook while in New Zealand and snorkel on the Great Barrier Reef when in Australia. I learned how to kayak off the coast of North Carolina and joined a hiking group in my hometown, where we have gorgeous park trails. I took a trip with a women's group to Idaho, where we bicycled every day and took yoga classes and bike repair lessons. Now, if I am cycling alone, I can fix my own flat.

I became more confident with each trip, more comfortable with traveling on my own. I realized I do not have to be married to travel well and often. I love my body, exactly as it is, and I am grateful for all the things I can do. I don't worry about what size I am, or how I look in my bicycle shorts. I did what a bumper sticker I saw advised: *Don't change the way you look; change the way you see.*

Journaling Prompts

- How do you feel about your body? Are you at war with it, always trying to change its shape? Or are you grateful for this body that serves you every day?
- Brainstorm a list of at least 20 ways to move your body. Set a goal to do at least one per day for 30 days. Journal daily about this.
- Create your own body-positive mantra. One of mine is: *I exercise daily because it adds power to my body and frees my mind.*

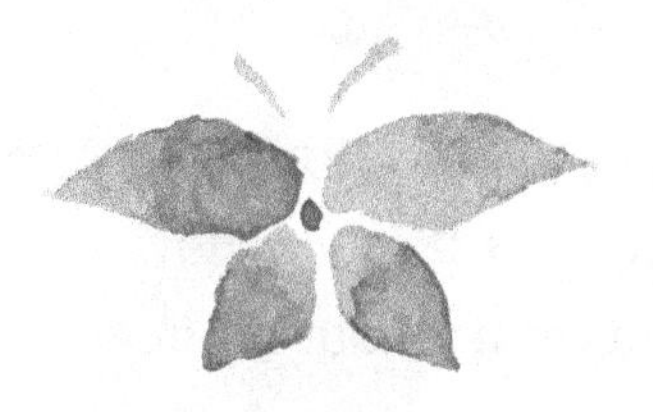

Chapter 7

Manage Your Money

When negotiating divorce, money is where the gloves come off and the bare-knuckle fighting begins. Divorce means a loss of money, money that once was yours. Money feels related to power and control, and because of that your ex may try to take as much as he can, especially if there is either a mistress or a new wife in the equation. Even if you are one of the lucky ones and your assets are divided equally (note I said equally, not fairly), you may need to make some changes in your lifestyle: how you plan, save, and spend. How you think about money.

Some of the problem is just math. You had one household supported by two incomes. Now there will be two households to support. Furthermore, the reality is the money will *not* be divided fairly. You might be living in the exact same place, with the exact same expenses, but have less than half the income to support it. The glib solution is to change your circumstances. But what if, for example, you have children who are settled in their schools and their activities? Do they have to pay a price for their parents' divorcing? Whatever your situation, it is difficult to uproot if you have lived somewhere a long time and have all your connections and relationships in that neighborhood. You may have your commute perfectly timed, your childcare network in place. You may be within walking distance of church or your favorite exercise class. But post divorce you may now be in a house that stretches the budget to near breaking. Once the divorce is finalized, no matter how badly or nicely you may have been treated, it is time to create your own money story.

To do that, you have six steps ahead of you: know your financial standing, review your money story, develop a healthy money mindset, select your money tribe, see money as energy, and make a five-year money plan.

Know Your Financial Standing

Once the dust has settled and you know your annual income, it is time to take advice from Elvis and take care of business. The first order of business is clarity. Know the exact amounts of your assets and your liabilities. Look closely at your income and expenses. Exactly how much do you have and how much do you need? If the have is less than the need, it is a crisis situation and demands change in either your needs–cutting back expenses–or your haves–increasing your income. Even if your spouse was the one who managed the money, you now have the reins. This is not optional; this is a must-do.

It is human for anger and resentment to pop up at this point. The easiest way to get past that is by taking control. You had a life and thought it was financially set, and now it isn't. Now you have this life and in this life you are in control. That is both empowering and a bit terrifying. The good news is that you will relish the serenity you have once you know exactly what money you have and how it is working for you, and establish a plan to acquire more security going forward.

Start with a system for tracking your money. If you like Excel, do a budget that way. If you prefer something more old-school, use pen and paper. If you like computer programs, try Quicken or search for a free program. Once you get the hang of this, you will feel the ease of having everything at your fingertips. Knowledge is power. By being a good steward of your money, you will have abundance.

Review Your Money Story

Let's look back for a moment to see what happened during your marriage. Who made more? Who controlled the money? Was the money situation transparent? Did you budget and plan expenditures together? Who had the final say or did you make joint decisions? If you had financial advisors, did the advisors always consult with you both or was he the "go-to" money person? Was there trust?

Once my ex started to make real money, he offered to take over paying the bills and managing the money. I agreed. I had been doing it through the lean years and didn't particularly enjoy it. Now we had more money to manage, and he had the resources through his law firm to manage it. I knew we had plenty of money, we talked over larger investments, and he agreed with my desire to be debt-free.

All was well financially until his affair was exposed. My trust had been misplaced. He was so confident that I wouldn't check up on him that he used our joint credit card to pay for things for the other woman. Once the affair was discovered, he established what he called a business account. Supposedly to keep his business expenses all in one place. I was not fooled; when I examined his "business" checkbook, I found thousands of dollars' worth of checks written to his mistress or to pay her bills. End of trust; marital money story changed. From that point until we divorced, I was in charge of the bills, and all investment meetings were held with both of us present.

As in most marriages, there was an income disparity in ours. I was the lower earner. I was a teacher, and I worked in inner-city schools with the poorest of the poor. He was a partner in a law firm, so he was with the richest of the rich. I think I felt that our life had some karmic balance to it. And he sort of mouthed along that he believed that too, but when we were divorcing there were all kinds of manipulations about what he deserved and what I did. He used every bit of the legal education that I made possible to limit what I had access to, to take what he felt was his. Although I worked every bit as hard as he did, I made less than 20% of what he did; at divorce, he felt he was entitled to more because he was earning more. Take some time to look back at your marital money story. Maybe write out the answers to the questions posed. Decide how you want that to change now that you can write your own story.

Develop a Healthy Money Mindset

Let's talk about money mindset. I've already shared that my ex and I brought different money histories to the marriage. There was a discrepancy between us in terms of upbringing, in terms of the money ideas we each brought to our married life. My parents were not well-educated; both had high school equivalency degrees. They worked hard, never spent more than they earned, managed to save, and considered debt intolerable. If they did not have the money for something, they didn't buy it. If there was something they wanted, they saved for it. When they finally bought a house, when I was 12, it had a 15-year mortgage. They paid it off in seven years. I never felt deprived as a child, though looking back I can see that money was tight.

In contrast, my ex's parents were both college-educated with excellent jobs. They lived in a beautiful house on a lake, with a mortgage, and always had new cars, often leased. In contrast to my never feeling deprived, my ex grew up with concerns about having enough money. We discovered our different money histories via taking a Suze Orman quiz.

We agreed, in our marriage, to be financially more like my parents than his. I did not need the fanciest house in the trendiest neighborhood. I was perfectly happy buying a used car and keeping it until it wore out. I was in favor of saving and avoiding debt. As a result of our agreement, we were financially solvent. When the firm where he had just purchased a partnership went under, we were inconvenienced, but nothing about our life had to change. This was in stark contrast to many of his partners, who were living on the edge without savings and had suddenly lost income.

Although he had more money growing up, he felt lack, felt insecurity. I had less but I felt I had everything I needed and more. My parents gave me the gift of possibility. I never doubted that I would go to college and I never expected for one second that my parents would pay for it. I literally worked my way through college. And I literally worked my ex's way through law school. The second he was finished, we began to pay off the loans incurred for the balance of his tuition. We devoted most of my teaching salary to paying that off. Because, well, debt is not good. We were in agreement on that.

As I explored my feelings post-divorce, I realized I was unsure about my making more money. This exposed a mindset issue that was standing in the way of my earning expectations. As a teacher, you are programmed to feel that it is all about the kids and not about you or money, that it is shallow to do something just for the money. Teachers never measure their worth in salary. By contrast, my ex once shared with me that he had a goal to be making six figures by a few years into his practice. I was stunned–it never occurred to me to have that kind of dollar goal. Perhaps you have similarly mixed feelings. Perhaps you are wondering what your earning potential is as you divorce.

Making money can be spiritual in that, when you have more money, you can do more, give more, help more. It is not selfish to want to earn money or shallow to be money-conscious. The more you care for money, the more money cares for you. The more attention you pay, the more you have to share.

The second mindset change you may need to make is around worth. When my ex and I divorced we had no debt–no mortgage, no school loans, nothing. We were totally financially solvent, and that had to do with my good money planning, my willingness to live modestly, my insistence on having the money before you buy something and paying off any debt as quickly as possible. I was essentially punished for this in the divorce because I had to justify expenses to determine alimony. I had continued to live modestly, and because of that my ex claimed I didn't need money from him. *She has no debt and lives below her means. She doesn't need more.* It did not occur to him that what I do with my marital money is my business and my low cost of living did not determine what I had contributed to the marriage. I had to fight to change my money mindset about my personal worth. Women often feel like they have been placed in the bargain bin at the time of divorce. That mindset needs to go.

Select Your Money Tribe

Once you have gotten a handle on your financial picture, it is time to start managing your money. You need at least two people on this team: a financial advisor and an accountant/tax preparer. Do not tell yourself your assets are too small to warrant these expenses.

If this seems like an intimidating task, there are several things you can do to prepare. First, do some reading. I very much recommend the books of Suze Orman and Kate Northrup. Orman's book *The Nine Steps to Financial Freedom* is the source of the survey I took with my husband exposing underlying money beliefs. Kate Northrup's book *Money: A Love Story* is an especially good place to start if you feel you are behind the eight ball financially. Take your time and read widely until you reach a comfort level. Check your local library and ask if they have any classes scheduled on financial planning or if the librarian can recommend some books.

Once you have some basic knowledge, start asking your friends who their financial advisors are and whether they would recommend them. Ask bluntly if the return on investment has been good. Then schedule a few appointments and listen to the financial advisors' pitches about what they can offer you. Remember your power here. You are the client; they work for you. Find someone you both feel comfortable with and trust. You can always change your mind and move your money elsewhere if they do not meet your expectations. Do the same thing to find an accountant or tax preparer. I truly love my accountant and my financial advisor. I trust them and rely on them.

Understanding Money as Energy

Let's talk about money as energy. Seeing money as another form of energy helps you see how fluid it is. As we exchange money, we are exchanging energy. We can also have energetic exchanges with other things that I believe fall into a larger category of abundance.

I note whenever abundance comes into my life, however small. Sometimes it is money or something with a high monetary value. Other times it might be a low monetary value but a lovely energetic reward. The more I notice these things, the more abundance I receive.

While straightening a drawer, I found three postage stamps, obviously a low money value. But I needed some stamps, I had something important to mail, and would have had to go to the post office. Now, no need! I simply put those three stamps on my large envelope and left it out for the postman to pick up. I write these abundances in my bullet journal. The first month I did it, I probably jotted down about 20 times when I noticed abundance. My most recent month was three pages long in tiny writing, and I know I did not get everything down. The more I notice, the more I receive.

Let's go back to those postage stamps. The day after I found them, I had to pay about $1,100 for a plane ticket to a coaching conference. I was not sure where to find that money. In the mail (remember those stamps?) I got a letter regarding an investment I own. There had been some unexpected dividends, and yes, it was enough money to pay for that plane ticket. No need to find the money elsewhere, it was delivered by stamped U.S. mail. Try paying attention to and expressing gratitude for the energetic abundance in your life. Then be prepared, because more and more will come your way.

Even situations that seem like the opposite of abundance may surprise you. After my divorce, I was still living in the house my husband and I had shared. He was demanding I put it on the market to get "his" money out of it, but my mother, who was under hospice care, was living with me. There was no way I could deal with a realtor or house showings or moving if the house sold quickly. So I bought him out. I let him set the price and just went to the bank and got a mortgage. You already know how I felt about debt–it was disheartening, honestly somewhat traumatic, for me.

But after my mother died and her estate was settled, my inheritance was sufficient to pay off the balance due on that mortgage. The evening after I went to the bank and wrote the check to pay off the house, I took the trash to the curb for pickup. I stopped and looked back at my home, the one I had just paid for a second time, and was filled with love and gratitude for it. I thanked it and said, *You are my safe place now, all mine and all paid for*, and I reveled in the peace and security of that. I was grateful that I had received an abundance in the form of an inheritance from my mother. The combination of that and my paying extra principal each month rid me of that debt. This house is filled with that energy and love. That is abundance!

As you shift from worrying about money to noticing and appreciating the energetic abundance in your life, more and more will come to you.

Your Five-Year Money Plan

Now take a leap of faith. Plan your income for the next five years. If you want to increase it significantly, put down the dollar amounts you desire and begin to think about how you will manifest that. Think about what you want to do to attract that money. I am not talking about buying a lottery ticket. I am talking about looking at your own talents, strengths, and skills and thinking about how they can bless and benefit you.

Then take the next step and construct your budget for each of those five years. Note your increasing income, your new assets, what you are acquiring, your budgets for travel and other good things, and where and in what amount you will be making ever-increasing donations.

My favorite quote, attributed to George Eliot, is: *It is never too late to be what you might have been*. It is not lost on me that George Eliot is the pen name for Mary Ann Evans. Thankfully, today, we can operate as women both artistically and in the financial world. The time is now to create your new money story!

Journaling Prompts

- Write your new money mantra. For example: *Money flows easily to me and I manage it well for the good of all.*
- *I deserve [insert your annual wish amount] because I…*
- *Today I experienced the energy of money as…*

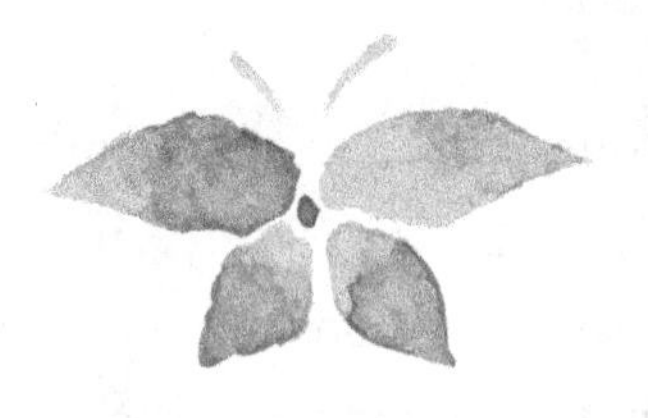

Chapter 8

• • • • • • • • • •

Discover Your Tribe

When you make the transition from married to single, it's not just the relationship between you and your husband that changes. Sometimes your relationship with his extended family becomes strained. Your relationship with your friends who are couples will shift. You will also have relationships change with regard to work. You will no longer be a part of his work gatherings, so those friends will fall away. Your entire social network will change. All the things that you did together... now you don't.

You have lost your constant companion. No one else will know the references, the inside jokes, the conversational history that you had together. It can feel lonely. You are used to being half of a couple and doing most things not just with another person, but with him. You have to learn how to be alone. So you need to start by being a tribe of one.

Learning how to be a tribe of one is an excellent self-care practice. When people asked me about when I was going to start dating, I would reply, "I already have–I'm dating me!" Before you dive into another relationship, give yourself the gift of getting to know who you are now. Perhaps during all those married years you'd been doing a lot of things because they were things he wanted to do. Now you have a complete blank slate. You can now design your own day, schedule your activities based on what you find pleasurable, what you find fun. How do you want to prioritize your time?

Try going some places alone that you might not have before. Start small by going out to lunch alone; when you are comfortable, try going out to dinner or to the movies by yourself. If there is a play you want to see and no one else is available, find out if there's a single seat open and take it.

You may imagine some weird glimpses and responses from people at first. You might think they feel pity for you or sad that you are alone. But they might be thinking, *Lucky lady, she's got some time for herself.* The more you learn to enjoy your own company, the more self-confident you will feel and appear. If you are happy with your own company, you don't need a date. If you are happy with your own company, then when you add someone–if you add someone–it's a bonus. You are complete on your own, and anyone additional is simply extra pleasure. I can assure you that, when you have this comfort and confidence with yourself, not only are others attracted to you, but you'll realize how delicious and empowering it can be to be alone.

What if you aren't comfortable being on your own and would like to go places with someone else? Or you are comfortable with being solo but would like the occasional company of a gentleman friend? Where do you find someone?

You already know some single women. You may not have spent much time with them socially because you were in a crowd of couples, but they're out there. Perhaps someone you know from work or from church or temple. Take the initiative, and ask friends or acquaintances to see a movie, meet for drinks after work, or take a class together. Classes are perfect in so many ways: you will be exploring something you are interested in with people who share that interest. You don't really need a friend to take the class or pursue an interest with you; you'll meet new friends there. Think wine tastings, restaurant dine-arounds, art gallery openings, meet-the-author nights at bookstores, ski clubs, hiking clubs, tennis or pickleball leagues–the choices are endless.

If you want to meet a potential partner, there are singles groups. If you want to spend some time with men but not necessarily date, maybe try a dance club or a dining-out group. If you are interested in dating, there are church or temple groups, community singles groups, and online dating resources. I don't really consider dating part of tribe building, but you may need a wing person as you explore the dating circuit, and that is someone to recruit from your tribe. Just be aware of the purpose in this situation; you are looking for a partner and so is your friend. Work out in advance what happens if one of you meets someone and wants to leave with him. Be sure you each have either another person around or prearranged plans to get home. Also have a check-in system in place in case something goes amiss after you separate.

You may need some new extended family in your tribe, some of the friends you considered family while part of a couple may drift away. You will likely not be invited to couples' evenings–an extra woman is not really welcomed in certain social circles. Or perhaps your ex has remarried and the couples have drawn her into the fold. You might still get invited out for a girls' lunch or shopping trip but soon the new wife will be part of those outings and that might become awkward. You may get a lot of promises about getting together but the invitations rarely materialize. Then you know for sure: it's time for a new tribe.

One of the potential bonuses of building a new tribe is developing some new pursuits. Maybe you spent a lot of time going with your spouse to, say, sporting events, even though they weren't your favorite thing to do. Now is the time to honor *your* first choices. If it's theater, consider volunteering at a theater. Or try out for a play. If you don't want to act, you could do sets or programs, or costumes. Be like Shawna.

Shawna loved theater. In college she had small parts in several productions and would occasionally pitch in on set construction. When talking about making choices for her new life as a single woman, she wistfully recalled those times. When we checked the local paper, there was an announcement that a small local theater was having auditions. It was a musical production, and Shawna does not sing, but with some encouragement she volunteered to help with sets and costuming. She loved the camaraderie of the theater group. They were happy to have her help, and she ended up with a small walk-on part. Now she volunteers regularly with the organization and has acted in several productions. Some of her closest friends came from doing this. She definitely considers theater folks her tribe.

I was interested in walking, so I joined Team in Training, an organization that raises money for leukemia research by having their athletes gather donations for each event. I met men and women dedicated to both endurance walking and running and supporting a good cause. We met twice a week to do increasingly longer distances as we prepared for events. After Saturday sessions, we'd go out for coffee or lunch depending on how long we'd trained. I felt like these people had my back. They taught me how to buy the appropriate shoes and socks and how to deal with chafing. You get pretty close to people when you share chafing cures! Plus, the walkers were also the talkers! You can get to know everyone's story as you walk together. It became a big extended family for me.

You can develop as many new circles as you like or need. I was participating in several 12-step groups, and, while the meetings are anonymous, folks often get together socially afterward. These were men and women who understood what I was going through. They were safe people with whom to let out all the feelings and fears and anger and grief. And they were funny! People who have hit rock bottom do not take themselves or their problems too seriously and know the healing power of laughter.

The important thing here is to remember who you are: a vibrant, desirable, funny, caring, bright, lively, gentle–or however you'd describe your strengths–person. Remember that anyone who spends time with you is blessed. Your time is precious, and you can now actively seek out people worthy of that time.

You now have the opportunity to spend some time getting a massage, going to more yoga classes, taking some more time to shop, to do lunch more often, and to do it at a tea shop if you feel like it. It is time to embrace this finding of your new tribe as a blessing and an expansion.

Reclaiming travel was key for me. I have wanderlust and was bitterly disappointed to lose my travel partner just as we had the time and money to go places. The easiest way for me to begin solo travel was to make it business-related. First as a writer, and then as a life coach, I signed up for retreats and conferences, domestic, then international. I learned to use Airbnb and met delightful hosts in the cities where I stayed. I made friends during the events and then sometimes found someone to share the expense of a room with the next time around. If you're a university graduate, check with your alumni office for some local gatherings or travel opportunities. Numerous travel companies and cruise lines offer singles or activity-oriented cruises. My local chamber of commerce offered incredible, reasonably priced trips, and I met so many folks that way. My in-town tribe increased exponentially.

You have a choice here. You can withdraw and allow your circle of friends to become smaller, cultivating fewer but deeper relationships. You can expand your reach, trying new things and creating multiple circles of friends. It depends on your personality and your desires. The emphasis here is on *your*. You are creating your life; the choices and the possibilities are endless.

Journaling Prompts

- Think back to before you were married. Name three things you did then that you don't do now.
- Why did you like those things? How did they make you feel?
- Choose one, or more, and write an action plan to try the activity again.

Chapter 9

Create New Traditions

What's the big deal about holidays? Well, holidays can be landmines on the road to a new life. Let's use two holidays as examples: Christmas and Valentine's Day.

Christmas is brutal. The first advertisements appear before Halloween. For at least two months we are immersed in a bath of commercials, programs, and specials focused on Christmas and Christmas traditions.

Everyone is singing, baking, buying and wrapping presents, planning and attending holiday parties–as couples, of course.

During your marriage your celebrations intertwined with your ex's. You learned the traditions from his family of origin and he learned yours. Together you created traditions that were unique to you as a couple and embedded into the lives of your friends and extended families. Each year together your traditions grew and expanded and became predictable. While different friendships and business relationships (think office parties) moved in and out of your lives, the two of you were the constant. If you look at most peoples' photo collections, many of the pictures are holiday shots. You can watch yourselves age, note where you lived and how your tastes changed. Your holiday history is your marriage history. Full of remembering when and *What a day that was* and *Oh, I remember that.*

Divorce changes it all. Some people are fortunate enough to have a civil relationship and work through the various holidays with ease and grace. Others are not so fortunate, and every single holiday becomes a pain point around what is no more.

I'm going to share some traditions from my marriage and how I changed them to reflect my new life. If you can lean into this, you will find the holiday stress defused and again be able to embrace these days. Let's find those landmines, disarm them, and plant flowers in the empty spaces.

I'll use decorating the Christmas tree as an example. On my first Christmas as a married woman, my mother gave me an ornament, a small horsehair pear. I'd seen it before, noticed it on our trees growing up, but was puzzled as to why she wanted me to have it. It had signs of age, was a bit fuzzy and faded, but she handed it to me as if she were giving me a precious gem. My mother was loving but not overly expressive about emotion, so this got my attention. She shared that her mother gave her the ornament for her tree in her first year of marriage, and now she wanted me to have it for my first tree. I was deeply touched and vowed that would be the first ornament we put on our tree every year.

I kept that promise. At first our trees had a collection of shiny balls bought on sale at K-Mart, fancied up with icicles and some tacky garlands. Each year we added a few ornaments that marked what was going on in our lives. Friends often gave us an ornament as a Christmas gift. The balls and garlands were replaced by teacher ornaments, gifts from my students. There was a set of decoupage wooden ornaments that I made while struggling with homesickness and loneliness the first year we lived away from our hometown. We added more ornaments each year: from the universities we attended, cities we visited, sports we were trying or following. The collection grew, and soon there were boxes full of ornaments, each carefully wrapped and labeled. Decorating the tree gave us a chance to look back at our life together. Whenever anyone visited our home, they often remarked on how heavily laden the tree was and would ask about specific ornaments. It wasn't just a tree; it was a record of our history together.

The first year my ex was out of the house I was determined to keep that tradition alive. It had been his job to get the tree out and assemble it and string the lights. Then we would add the ornaments together, laughing and appreciating our life story. That year, my goddaughter and I hauled the tree up together and managed to get the lights on. I still made certain that pear was the first ornament on, but it broke my heart.

Although my parents had difficulties in their marriage, they never parted, never gave up on one another. I felt like a failure, but I had not yet given up on our reconciliation so placing each ornament on the tree that year was an act of faith and hope. How could anyone walk away from such a rich and varied life?

As the years of separation passed, it became harder to do this. Christmas Day, once a source of family love and gratitude, became a lonely day. Something had to change.

The first Christmas after my divorce, I chose to celebrate the winter solstice. I invited a group of women to my home. I had my tree up, but by then I was not putting all the ornaments on; it was just too painful. My ex had walked away, never bothered to even ask about any of them. It felt to me like he was just dumping all those memories and traditions, that they held no meaning, no importance for him. I felt the opposite way–they were painful to me because they represented loss. It was a struggle to accept that what I found so precious meant so little to my life partner. But I still put that pear on first and then added pinecones and acorns, representing the seeds of my future.

I created a completely new tradition. I asked each woman to come prepared to share what it was she wanted to leave in the dark on this, the longest night of the year. I created a ritual. I asked each to choose a word to represent what she was drawing to herself as the light returned. We formed a circle, each woman holding a candle, and I lit my candle and then passed the light around the circle. We took turns sharing what we desired to leave behind and what we were embracing. To close the circle, I promised that I would hold all of their intentions in my heart throughout the year. And it was magical. The energy in the room was palpable.

I'd planned a craft activity. I collected catalpa seedpods, and I asked each of them to write their word onto two pods, one for them to take with them and one to leave with me. We shared a simple dinner I had made–chili, fresh bread, and salad. These women had been so honest and brave in their sharing. Not all of them knew one another; their connection was that they were friends of mine from all parts of my life. I kept those pods in a basket near my desk, and every time I saw it, I thought of them and their intentions. I have continued this practice ever since. Most guests share that it is one of their favorite nights of the year.

Over the years, Christmas has become less and less important to me. I don't put up a tree, but I do decorate my fireplace mantel, and my mother's pear still goes on there first. I honor her and my parents' long marriage. I honor myself and the seeds still spreading in my life with a scattering of acorns and pinecones among the greenery. More important to me is a collection of stones, one from every year I have celebrated the solstice with my women friends. Each stone has one of my guide words on it, and I can track my new life through those words just like I used to track my life through the ornaments on the tree. I created a rich tradition that honors my life choices and reminds me how blessed I am to have these powerful and generous women in my life. December is not filled with emotional landmines any longer. Instead it is a time of richness and creativity.

The goal is to take a holiday that might be a trigger for loss, a reminder of what you no longer have, and make it into a day that speaks to you and what you love. You don't have to give up everything. I've kept alive some other Christmas traditions from my past but tailored them to my current situation. It is empowering to make these days your own. Take and make joy!

Karen struggled with the sharing of her teenage children during Christmas. The original agreement was that, on alternating years, one parent would have Christmas Eve and the other would have Christmas day. She hated this. The time with the kids felt rushed and awkward, the time without them was hard to fill because her friends were busy with their own holiday traditions. The kids didn't adjust well either–too much moving back and forth in too short a time period.

We decided to explore other solutions. Karen sat with her feelings and asked herself what she really wanted. The answer was for herself and her children to have a relaxed and peaceful holiday. She asked herself, could she have a Christmas without them and if so, what would that look like? Could they have Christmas without her? She felt a surprising amount of ease around this possibility. When she talked with her children, after an initial barrage of questions, they embraced the idea of switching off, being with each parent every other Christmas.

But what would she do on the Christmases when her children were with their dad? She pondered the idea of going to either her parents' or a sibling's house, but that felt unsatisfying. She decided to celebrate being alone by doing exactly what she wanted to do, to take the holiday and do something she loved. Now, every other year Karen plans her perfect getaway. One year she made a reservation at a resort where she had room service, a massage, and all the yoga classes her heart desired. One year she rented a cabin so she could curl up with a stack of books and a bottle of good wine. One year she joined a small group of women on a "hiking the holiday" trip. She doesn't rule out spending her no-kids holiday with her extended family, but only if she chooses, honoring her desires and needs. And the years she has the children? Those are much more relaxed and happy. They are currently considering planning a holiday trip together, inspired by how their mom does Christmas when not with them.

Valentine's Day is another difficult holiday for divorced women. Weeks and months before February 14th, the television, radio, and newspapers are filled with advertising the celebration of love. The diamond commercials alone are constant reminders that a woman's worth is reflected in the kind of gift her partner delivers. Restaurants are booked up weeks in advance, and it is one of the busiest times of year for florists. My ex always gave me a lovely gift, usually jewelry. There was always a sweet card as well. Then suddenly, no valentines were coming my way. He was in another relationship and I was not. It was still hard for me to even imagine being with someone else. So what to do?

I got creative again. I invited ten women friends to my home on Valentine's Day night. Some were single. Some were divorced. Some had husbands who were total duds in the romance department. I explained that I was not going to be cooking but there would be plenty of wine and chocolate and I would order in pizza. The purpose of the night was to celebrate us as women. The only requirement was to buy a gift for herself. I asked each woman to think carefully about what her heart desired and then buy exactly that. It could be big or small, expensive or inexpensive, didn't matter. What mattered was that it be exactly what she longed for most. I asked her to wrap the present as beautifully as she desired and bring it to the party.

What an amazing night we had. Each woman opened her gift as we all oohed and aahed. The best part was listening to the explanation each woman shared for why she chose what she did and why she deserved it. The gifts were not the traditional lingerie and jewelry. Well, there was one set of absolutely spectacular lingerie, bought by a woman we would never have expected to go for that. We cheered for her when she said something like, *I always wanted lingerie like this and I am going to wear it just for myself, to make me feel beautiful.* One woman bought herself a card that contained a gift certificate for a local home improvement store. Included in the card were paint chips and photographs of the new cabinets and kitchen counters she wanted. This woman was treating herself to a kitchen makeover. Her husband had been balking about it for years, and she decided she deserved a new kitchen, had waited long enough, and gave it to herself. We stood and applauded her. Some women bought themselves books and magazine subscriptions. One woman bought herself a power drill! The beauty of this new celebration was that it was still about love. We were practicing self-love and demonstrating love and affirmation for one another, complete exactly as we are, without regard for relationship status. It was liberating to break out of the *Valentine's Day is for couples only* mindset.

Journaling Prompts

- What holidays are most difficult for you since your divorce?
- What new way can you create to celebrate those days?
- Who can you enlist to help with this project?

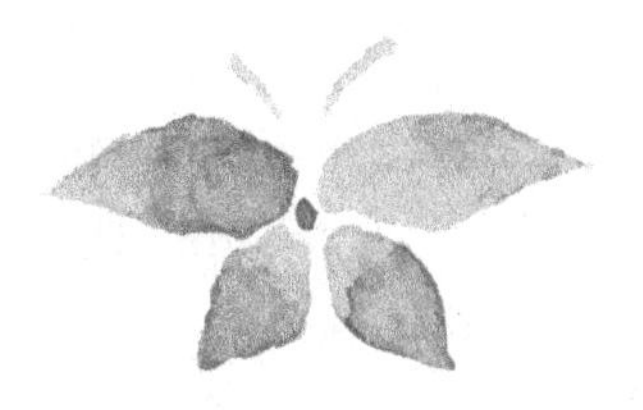

Chapter 10

Re-Story Your Life

Once I stopped looking at my marriage through either a haze of pain or rose-colored glasses, once I began to look at me instead of the marriage, once I completed my marriage autopsy and allowed myself to retrieve the good, I realized that it was in my marriage that I achieved my first bloom. I saw my strengths and my weaknesses and accepted them all as glorious parts of me. Most importantly, I began to find the joy in creating something new, a life uniquely designed for me, by me. The freedom of that was exhilarating. Every step on the journey you have taken thus far has led you here, the beginning of your second bloom.

My new story is writing and life coaching. The arc between these two things is my desire to help other women, to help someone experiencing a midlife divorce get through it easier and faster than I did.

The writing came first. Because I had journaled most of my life and because it was one of my lifelines through my most wretched moments; I leaned into writing. I joined an organization called the Story Circle Network and in a small online group began to share tiny snippets, just a few hundred words, about my life. I found community and encouragement there. I didn't write just about the betrayal and divorce. Because they provided a monthly prompt, I wrote about my mother and dad, my school, my son, my hopes and dreams. Those stories grew into essays and I gathered the courage to begin to write a memoir. When the memoir felt too big to tackle, I did a course correction, began to write personal essays, and found a literary home there. While taking classes to learn writing craft, I tried my hand at fiction and realized how freeing it was to be in complete charge of how the story unfolds. It was through fiction that I first began to re-story my own life. Every November I participate in NaNoWriMo–National Novel Writing Month. You write 50,000 words in 30 days, a first draft. During those months over the course of several years, I crafted a book of personal essays, the first version of my memoir, and the bones for two novels in a series and a Christmas story that I just know will be a made-for-TV movie one day.

Because I was a teacher and had done staff development, I designed a writing seminar called Legacy Writing. It is a six-week course in which beginning writers craft and polish one story into print for their friends and families. I developed a class on Writing Mindset.

This is how the second part of my dream to help other women crystallized. My therapist and writing mentors suggested I think about life coaching. When I realized it could mean working with women one-on-one or in small groups, helping them develop the skills and confidence to name and pursue their dreams, I felt that frisson, that deep knowing, that this was my path.

I invited my first group of Legacy Writing students to my home to celebrate their "publication," distributing the bound collection of their stories. What a thrill to watch the joy of having a "first book" in hand. That night, I shared this new and very tender life-coaching dream of mine. I asked if any of them knew about life coaching and if they thought I might be good at it. To my utter astonishment, two of the women had recently worked with life coaches, and both they and the others in the group encouraged me. *Yes,* they said, *you could do that and you will be good at it.* See how the universe lined that up for me? I became a life coach, adding that to my way of helping others through.

I had been coaching in one way or another for years; it was a through-line in teaching and writing. One sunny day as I was journaling about my coaching practice, I looked up and noticed the amaryllis plant near the window. The plant was a gift from a friend and had bloomed in a spectacular fashion. Once it ceased blooming, I had stopped noticing it. That tall first bloom had withered and was drooping downward, but right next to it was a strong shoot with a second bloom on top ready to burst into its glory. At that moment I knew what my coaching business name was: Second Bloom!

My first plan was to write personal essays and memoir to share my experience to help other women. My first writing goal was essays in literary magazines, and I achieved that, winning some awards and scholarships along the way. The long-term goal was a memoir, which is a work-in-progress. I tucked away an additional dream to publish fiction, showing women a range of new happy endings.

Now coaching fills my life with bliss. The beauty of coaching is that it is interactive, and for an extrovert like myself that is a dream come true. I assist women on their paths to a new life. Assisting other women, coaching them as they create the life of their dreams gives me joy and I am so grateful to be able to do this.

This book is the embodiment of the connection between my writing and coaching. I took a leap of faith, learning a new writing genre. Self-help books are written differently than memoir or fiction but draw in a way from both. This book is my love letter to women poised to recreate their lives, ready to craft their second blooms.

Re-storying your life is like fiction writing. You choose the characters, you create the plot, and you design the finish. It's also like personal essay and memoir in that the building blocks, the growth lessons from your life, are there for you to draw upon.

One of Steven Covey's seven principles is "begin with the end in mind." So let's pick an end point to plan toward. Let's start to re-story your life now. One caveat: allow room for surprises, gifts from the universe. Name your dream, lay down your plans, take bold action toward them. And at the same time keep an open mind, allow for more.

I am indebted to Angela Lauria for the inspiration for this next exercise. Angela, the book maven who founded the Author Incubator, in one of our coaching sessions tossed out the idea of writing your bio from five years hence. Brilliant! I believe that putting your dreams down on paper is the first step toward actualization. But, as Dr. Phil frequently advises, you have to put some verbs in the sentences.

First, settle into the idea of a five-year leap. Write down the year and your age then. Now visualize your ideal future life. Brainstorm in these areas: family, friends, relationships, health, career, wealth, lifestyle, and achievements. Where do you live? Who's with you? What are you giving to the world? What are your current goals and pursuits? What is your current dream?

Now write a third-person biography for yourself at that time. Hold nothing back! Dream big because this is the you to come.

Conclusion

• • • • • • • • • • •

What Now?

"And the day came when the risk to remain tight in a bud was more painful than the risk it took to blossom."
–Anaïs Nin

I love this quote because I lived it. The day came when I just had to step out of the fear, step out of my comfort zone, be brave, and blossom. Perhaps you were feeling this when you spotted the title *Post-Divorce Bliss*? Or perhaps it was the subtitle, "Ending Us and Finding Me"? Something resonated there for you, some inner knowing or inner desire to make this your season.

You followed that hunch, that curiosity, all the way to this point. There are several possible paths for you now.

What if you've read all the chapters, but you haven't done a single prompt? You haven't answered a single question, you haven't stretched your body in any new ways or joined any new groups. What if you haven't done anything to expand your tribe or recreate your life? What if at this moment you just want some time to process? You are pondering but not ready for action.

I want to give you a thumbs-up for reading all the way through. I want to give you a thumbs-up for thinking about what I've shared. I want to give you a thumbs-up for maintaining an open mind and heart. Maybe this is not the moment to make changes in your life. Maybe this is a moment for you to lie fallow, resting. But the seeds have been planted in your field of possibilities. When the moon is right, the season is right, the ground softens, and you are ready, the things you've read and subconsciously tucked away will split and something new will grow. This information will still be here when you are ready to take action. And I will be holding the intention that you will chase your heart's desire and capture it.

What if you have read through, noted the chapters that resonated with you and written to the journaling prompts in those chapters and felt a shift, felt change root in your soul? Right now, you want to live in this phase, this beginning for a while. You have felt a shift begin, and you desire to be where you are right this moment for a while. You want to let these changes, this shift, settle in. You have nurtured the seeds of change and are in a period of gestation. I encourage you to try some of the exercises you skipped. I urge you to take your writing and journaling to the next level. You have momentum. Keep engaging with your dreams, pursuing your passion, and following your intuition. I applaud you. I'm proud of you. I am grateful this book helped you and I wish you only the very best as you move forward on your journey. If I have played even a small part in facilitating that journey I am humbled and grateful.

What if you have turned more than a few pages, nodding your head and saying, "Me, too. I've experienced this too!" What if you've done most of the exercises and felt a sea change in your self and mindset? Your seeds have taken root, broken through the soil and have beautiful green leaves and numerous buds. You are filled with possibility. You are ready to burst into bloom. If that is you and you want to go deeper, do more, if you want to not waste another moment, please check out the last page in this book for a free gift and how to contact me at Second Bloom Coaching. We can discuss how to take you on a deep dive into planning and expanding your new life. You can have my assistance in crafting your second bloom.

I guess there is one other possibility: You could do nothing. You could keep yourself exactly where you are. You could stay stuck. Decide all of this is for someone else, not for you. But I doubt it. You found this book or someone found it for you. You took the time to read it all the way to the end. And I believe with all my heart that you are poised for your second bloom. You can do it!

Congratulations to all of my readers. Thank you for being gloriously you. Thank you for taking steps toward creating your best life. Turn to the last page in this book for that thank you gift from me. May we all thrive!

Jude Walsh
Second Bloom Coaching
www.secondbloomcoaching.com

Acknowledgments

Thank you first and foremost to the women who share their divorce journeys with me. It is truly bliss watching you thrive.

Thank you to my writing families:

- The Emporium NaNoWriMettes: Lori Gravley, Rebecca Morean, and Debra Wilburn.
- The Plot Sisters: Christina Consolino, Cindy Cremeans, Ruthann Kain, Jen Messaros, and Traci Ison Schafer.
- The Story Circle Network's Work-In-Progress Group

- Eric Maisel and The Deep Writing Workshop Writers
- The Antioch Writer's Workshop at the University of Dayton

Thank you to my coaching families:

- The Powerhouse Coaches
- The Author Incubator
- The Order of the Quill

Thank you to Angela Lauria for her sassy leadership and sterling example of moving forward always.

Thank you to my editor Cynthia Kane. I hope this is just the beginning of a long and fruitful collaboration.

Thank you to all the 12-step group members who taught me to take what I need and leave the rest.

Thank you to my Solstice Sisters for helping me move toward the light.

Thank you to Chris Gargasz, photographer extraordinaire.

Thank you Jed Diamond, Lori Gravley, Pam Styles, Mary Beane, Donna Andrew, Muriel Hunt, Barb

Kuvshinoff, Linda Vanarsdall, Rebecca Snapp, Kate Hennessey, and Claire Butler for always being on Team Jude.

To the Morgan James Publishing team: Special thanks to David Hancock, CEO & Founder for believing in me and my message. To my Author Relations Manager, Tiffany Gibson, thanks for making the process seamless and easy. Many more thanks to everyone else, but especially Jim Howard, Bethany Marshall, and Nickcole Watkins.

Biggest thanks and all my love to the best son in the whole wide world, Brendan.

About the Author

Jude Walsh tried to do everything right. She worked hard, earning bachelor's, master's, and doctoral degrees. She married her high school sweetheart and stood by his side as he followed his dreams. She gave up her Pennsylvania mountains to move with him to Ohio and learned to savor the prairie and wide skies. An educator, she taught students from preschool through the doctoral level and loved them all. Jude was in the best job of her life as the teacher coach in a school she co-founded with a group of visionary teachers when midlife divorce changed everything. The dreams she spent a lifetime nurturing ended abruptly and not by her choice.

After a lifetime as "us," she had to learn to live as "me." It was a heartbreaking and difficult path. As a longtime journaler, she turned to writing to make sense of her new reality. That led to writing memoir, personal essay, fiction, and even some poetry. Active in the literary community, her work has been published in numerous magazines and anthologies. She teaches Legacy Writing, a class she designed, to help people get their life stories into print for their families, and Writing Mindset. As a creativity and life coach, she savors helping women create their second bloom. Today she travels frequently, writes daily, and leans into the abundant adventure her life has become.

Jude is a writer and life coach dedicated to helping other women not just survive midlife divorce but thrive as they create a beautiful new reality. She lives with her son and three lively dogs in Dayton, Ohio.

Websites: www.secondbloomcoaching.com and www.judewalsh-writer.com

Facebook: SecondBloomCoaching

Thank You

I am grateful we had this time together and would be honored if you chose to stay in touch with me. You can reach me via email at jude@secondbloomcoaching.com and I will add you to my mailing list. I look forward to hearing about your second bloom and your journey toward creating a beautiful life post-divorce.

To thank you I'd like to offer you my master class *Common Mistakes Made After Divorce*. Please visit my website at www.secondbloomcoaching.com/FreeGift for a link to the class. Once you are on my mailing list you will be notified of future offerings.

The best truly is yet to come.

CPSIA information can be obtained
at www.ICGtesting.com
Printed in the USA
JSHW021653080622
26848JS00002B/206

9 781642 792348